The Power Of Mental Models

How To Make Intelligent Decisions, Gain A Mental Edge And Increase Productivity

By

Joseph Fowler

FREE BONUS!

Free Thinking Cheat Sheet Reveals...

21 timeless thinking principles you need to know to upgrade your thinking and make smarter decisions (not knowing these may hinder you from having the success you'd like to have in life)

CLICK HERE TO DOWNLOAD FOR FREE!

Or go to www.thinknetic.net or simply scan the code with your camera

Table of Contents

Introduction 8

Chapter 1: What Are Mental Models? .. 12
    Unforced Errors 19

Chapter 2: Why Do We Use Mental Models? 22
    How Are Mental Models Created? 26

Chapter **3:** Mental Models **In** Problem-Solving **32**
    Better Problem Solving 35

Chapter **4:** Decision-Making **With** Mental Models **39**
    Variety Matters 39
    Minimize Black And White Thinking 42
    Logic Vs. Emotions 44

Chapter 5: Factors That Define The Quality Of The Mental Model 50
    Flexibility 52

Competence 54

Multidisciplinary Approach 55

Inversion 57

First Principles 58

The Pareto Principle 59

Chapter 6: Biases And Heuristics 62

Availability 64

Regression To The Mean 65

Affect Heuristic 66

Overestimation Of Randomness 68

Representativeness 69

Anchoring And Adjustment 71

Recognition Heuristic 72

Rational Choice Theory 74

Less-Is-More Effects 75

Chapter 7: Most Used Mental Models . 78

Confirmation Bias 79

Disconfirmation Bias 81

Backfire Effect 82

Self-Serving Bias 83

Fundamental Attribution Error 85

Hindsight Bias 86

Dunning-Kruger Effect 87
Reciprocity Model 88
Optimism/Pessimism Bias...................................... 89
Negativity Bias 90
Optimistic Probability Biases................................. 92
Occam's Razor... 92
Hanlon's Razor.. 93
Forer Effect 94
Declinism 96
Nudging...97
Anchoring.. 99
Forcing Functions 100
Theory Of Constraints.. 101
The Tragedy Of The Commons 102
Certainty Effect 103
Framing..104
Time Discounting..106
Decoy Effect 108
Deterring Of Small Decisions...............................109
Sunk-Cost Fallacy 110
Survivorship Bias 111
Ostrich Effect 112

Salience 112

Placebo Effect.. 113

Recency 114

Pro-Innovation Bias 115

Clustering Illusion 116

Chapter 8: Cognitive Dissonance 118

What To Do 122

Forced Compliance 125

Decision-Making 125

Effort 127

Chapter 9: Reversible Vs. Irreversible Decisions 129

Think Outside The Box 133

Conclusion 140

References 144

Disclaimer 150

Introduction

Do you feel as if your mind is stuck on a track, and you can't redirect it however much you want to? Do you make bad decisions or limit yourself because of certain types of thinking? The culprit to your problems involves something known as mental models.

Mental models are simply frameworks that direct your thinking. Drawing from your past experiences and beliefs, your mind forms a default way of thinking that drives your decisions. This system is great in that it automates decision-making; imagine having to take the time to carefully think through a decision when you are about to get into a car accident and you must make a snap choice on how to avoid it!

But it is an imperfect system, as you are probably well aware of. Mental models can take away your ability to rationalize and make informed decisions because you are resorting to habit. You may not even realize that your decisions are based on mental models, which is why education on mental models is so helpful.

Learning about mental models is the first step to overcoming the hurdles that they can place before you in life. Once you understand how your own mind works, you will be better able to identify and address problematic mental models and cultivate better thinking and reasoning skills. This book will teach you everything you need to know, so that you can take control of your own mind and make life work for you.

I have spent over a decade studying psychology and the human mind. From my experience working and learning in psychology, I am quite familiar with how mental models work. I have developed a system to control my own thinking, which has elevated me to new heights in life. I wouldn't be where I am today if I kept engaging in the limiting and narrow thinking I used to default to. Drawing from this research, I am here to present an actual solution to problematic mental models as well as science-backed information about what mental models are and how they form.

You will gain an immense amount of self-control, willpower, and creativity by learning about mental models and how to harness them. You will be able to think outside of the box and take on new opportunities. You will be able to solve problems more creatively and efficiently by focusing on logic, not biases or emotions. The result is that you will have better relationships, more success at work, and more self-esteem. In addition, you can rid yourself of certain harmful mental models that work against you in life, causing poor self-esteem, depression, and other self-defeating issues.

Using real science, this book is the answer to your prayers because it actually teaches you about your mind and how to correct its unique idiosyncrasies. Most self-help books suggest positive thinking; but it can be nearly impossible to adopt positive thinking if your mental models prevent such an outlook. With the knowledge in this book, you can train your mind to do what you want and stop limiting you in all areas of life.

I promise that by the end of this book, you will have all of the tools necessary to become happier and more satisfied with your life. While I can't make you use these tools, you would be wise to. Your life will improve exponentially and you will find many barriers break down when you reroute your thinking.

You have spent all of your life resorting to your mental models. They comprise your reality. So why wait any longer to get started on better thinking and better living? Start reading today to learn how to become your best self by retraining your mind. The work is not necessarily easy, but it is worthwhile, so you should start today.

Chapter 1: What Are Mental Models?

What are these mental models of which I speak? I'm glad you asked because mental models are the foundation of your entire reality. Understanding them is critical to understanding yourself and your life.

Most people take reality at face value. They assume that life is as they see it. But the reality of reality is that it is subjective, based on each person's unique perception and imagination. A lot of factors go into shaping one's reality. The result is that no two people see anything the exact same way.

This leads to a lot of conflict in the world, but it can also lead to people making poor decisions based on limited understandings of the reality before them. Mental models are what you use to read reality and a problematic one can certainly make your life harder because it prevents you from seeing reality with clarity.

A mental model is a representation of the human mind's thought process [1]. Mental models are how we understand the world. Not only do they shape what we think and how we understand situations, but they drive our decisions and feelings [1]. They lay the entire basis for our lives. What makes mental models tricky is that they are not just influenced by reality – but rather, they draw from a series of experiences, biases, and even a person's current mood. Shaped by culture, personal experiences, and background, they are as unalike as snowflakes from person to person. Two children raised in the same household will have two very different mental models, despite having similar backgrounds and the same culture.

Everything that a person sees, hears, and otherwise senses are represented by mental models inside their minds [2]. Mental models are used as scales by which a person automates decisions and internalizes external stimuli. The Internal scales, as mentioned by scientists, are ever-changing and unstable as the human mind is susceptible to change due to adaptation. They are also variable since every person has a different outlook and thus a different set of models.

Mental models use perception to drive reasoning and decisions [1]. Obviously, this reasoning can be flawed at times. Every bit of reasoning you engage in is driven by your perception, no matter how erroneous it may be, as well as dozens or even hundreds of other factors that you may not be aware of.

For example, you may avoid spending time with someone who has a lot of tattoos because you were raised to believe that people with tattoos are lowlifes, but you are not aware of that bias and you simply dislike someone based on his body modifications. Meanwhile, another person would not have that bias because he was raised differently, so he has no problem hanging out with heavily tattooed people. Your mental model drives you to make a decision about a person that you may not even be consciously aware of.

Furthermore, mental models drive priorities [1]. One woman may consider getting her hair and nails done every few weeks an utmost priority, while another woman does not consider those things necessary at all. Your mental model helps you rate things based on importance so that you can dedicate time, money, and energy to something that you consider worthwhile. Not everyone will agree with your priorities because everyone has a different rating system for importance in life.

Mental models are imperfect because they are lacking complete information. Obviously, you can't know everything and focus on everything in the world [1]. You can only focus on a few tiny parts that fit into your accepted reality [1]. Therefore, your lens of reality is quite narrow and yet it shapes many decisions that can be quite huge.

Think about this example: You support a certain political healthcare proposal because you recognize a few problems, probably problems that affect you personally somehow, with the current system. You vote thusly. However, other people disagree with your accepted healthcare model because they see different problems with the model that you cannot see from your perspective. Thus, you don't understand why people disagree with you and you feel frustrated.

Your mind will create a small-scale model with the evidence it currently possesses for each situation it encounters [2]. This model will include predicted outcomes of each situation and each decision. Whether or not these outcomes are accurate is hard to say. Sometimes you are right; oftentimes you are wrong.

Mental models are paradoxical. Some are quite fluid and change with time and experience [3]. That is why you are a different person now than you were ten years ago, and twenty years ago, and so on. Over the course of your life, you begin to change mental models and adapt them to fit what you need from life. Yet, mental models are also incredibly rigid. Some stay with you for life. Others may be fluid, but your mind relies on them so heavily that it applies them to every area of life, even areas of life that don't benefit from the said mental model.

The takeaway here is that mental models can be changed and adapted to become more helpful. However, you must work hard on your mind to undo years of experience that has created the models. You must also perform some brutally honest introspection to uncover the true roots of certain thoughts and actions that you routinely engage in. You must be able to let your ego down for a second and say, "Hey, I'm not doing something right. I need to make a change."

Why is this mental work worthwhile? The fact is that your reasoning is not based on logic or rules, but rather mental models [4]. So if you are operated on a bad mental model, you are depriving yourself of the ability to use logic to arrive at the ideal decision. Your decisions are influenced in a direction that may not be beneficial in the long run, even though you think they are great decisions. Learning to recognize mental models and focus on logic instead can help you make the best decisions for yourself.

Also, since mental models vary from person to person, what works for you may not work for anyone else. This is why your decisions can create a lot of negative conflict within your family, your relationship, or your team at work. Learning to depend less on mental models can help you arrive at good decisions for everyone involved. This can help you become a better spouse, parent, and leader. It can also help you remove the emotion from decisions, which in turn can lessen the pain of having to compromise on a decision. Since all relationships contain a lot of compromise, you will do better in life if you are able to accept compromise.

Unforced Errors

An unforced error is basically a mistake or bad decision that somehow harms you. In sports, the mistake is often attributed to your own failure, rather than the talent of the opponent. For example, if you goof at a tennis match, you may blame yourself for not playing the right way when really you were up against a better tennis player.

The fewer unforced errors you make in life, the better off you are. You can avoid making grave errors at work or in your family. You can avoid entering harmful relationships or losing lots of money. Basically, things are great in life when you make wise, informed decisions.

Mental models are designed to help you avoid

unforced errors [5]. By using a first bias model, people tend to operate on loss aversion, or basically preventing losses, rather than using their skills for the maximum potential benefit [5]. Thus, most people have a built-in loss aversion model that drives them to make decisions in life, as represented by athletes' decisions in sports. This model is not ideal, however, as using your skills for maximum utility and focusing on making good decisions instead of minimizing losses is a better use of your energy.

Your brain has intuition, and nine times out of ten, that intuition is wrong. Many of our instincts no longer serve us, yet they run in the background, driving us to make decisions that don't make a lot of logical sense. It is wise to use your brain's intuition and mental models as a guide for life, not an instructional manual. If you have an intuitive response to a situation, be sure to check out your intuitive with logic before committing to the decision.

Since the brain absolutely loves to formulate predictions [2], you often think that you know how something will go. You then base your decision off of that assumption to avoid an unforced error. However, life is seldom that predictable. Take your assumptions as hypotheses, not reality.

Chapter 2: Why Do We Use Mental Models?

Since mental models are such an imperfect system of assumptions and hidden motives, why do we even use them? Wouldn't the brain have a more accurate way of making decisions?

The short answer is that no, the brain does not have a better way of rapidly processing data and reaching critical decisions. Mental models conserve time and energy, making them the most useful and sophisticated means of navigating reality. The example in the introduction about making a snap decision in a time of danger when you are facing an impending car accident illustrates how mental models can be extremely useful and even life-saving.

The long answer is that there is much complex neuroscience behind why mental models form and why we adhere to them religiously. While neuroscience is beyond the scope of this book, it is important to distinguish between two types of thinking that your brain uses, called System 1 and System 2 [6].

System 1 thinking is what uses the mental models [6]. It is a fast, almost intuitive way of making decisions. You look at the evidence and a mental model calculates what you must do in a matter of nanoseconds. Without putting a lot of energy into making a decision, you are able to conserve your energy for other things.

System 1 generates impressions and feelings, which influence your reactions. It acts quickly, automatically, and effortlessly by recognizing patterns (which may not actually exist), seeking coherence among ideas in your memory, and selecting the skills you must use in a given situation so that you can make a decision rapidly. It likes to default to the easiest answers, thinking that the data it can retrieve easily is the truth. This system is also primed to infer causes or intentions and make predictions. It can notice information that stands out because it doesn't have to dig very deep to retrieve that information. Finally, it ignores doubt and ambiguity, to make the decision-making process more automatic and less cumbersome or worrisome. Mental models help System 1 have a convenient route to essential information necessary to arrive at decisions quite unimpeded.

So, we use mental models created in our heads to solve most of the problems and make most of the decisions in our everyday routine, essentially creating shortcuts in our minds that minimize the effort spent on thinking.

System 2 is more arduous. It is a slow means of analyzing data and employing careful logic to arrive at an ideal decision. In work or relationships, System 2 is great. It is not so great when you are about to get into a car wreck. It also requires a lot of energy and time. This is because it must dig through your memory, look at facts from all angles, and do some research to arrive at a decision.

Even when you are not in times of duress, your brain prefers System 1 thinking. Thinking is metabolically expensive; 20% of our energy intake goes to the brain [7]. Since slow thinking is expensive, the body is programmed to avoid it. Your brain basically defaults to the faster way of thinking, making System 1 mental models a preferred method.

Moreover, despite what your teenager or boss tells you, dedicating energy to thinking about one thing means that energy is not available for other things. Multitasking is not possible or real [8]. As you split your attention between two things, you lose a little bit of dedication to both items. It is far better to focus on one thing at a time. System 1 makes it easier to hone in on one thing that it considers important, which in turn makes you overlook over important factors that you should consider when making a decision.

How Are Mental Models Created?

Starting the minute you are born, your brain starts to learn what it needs to create a mental model. Based on conditioning, it learns that certain situations lead to certain outcomes, and certain behaviors are rewarded or punished. For instance, you learned that when you cried, your mother held you and fed you. Thus, you learned to speak up when you needed something.

Over time, these ideas become cemented in the mind, forming a mental model that the mind defaults to. By a certain age, crying no longer got you what you wanted, so your mental model adapted to a different technique to get food and attention. Your mental models become adapted with time, but they remain in the background of your subconscious, driving your behavior and decisions to get desired results.

Mental models are also designed to help you navigate reality. You learn early on that you are supposed to stop a car when you see a red octagon sign, so now you do that automatically without thinking about it. Most mental models are not so simple, however. Through a similar process, you begin to form biases about how people are and how the world works based on a few immediately observable signs. Certain stimuli make you reach certain decisions that you treat as fact. For example, you learned that being overweight is bad so you secretly judge overweight people and you become hard on yourself if you become overweight.

The older you become, the more rigid your mental models are. Behaviors that have served you thus far become such habit that you may not even realize the mental models that drive them to exist. If you do nothing to change these mental models, they will persist. The brain does not see any reason to change, and it doesn't want to expend the effort, so it continues to rely on its default models without question.

Mental models are formed over time by the examples your role models and peers set, by the media, and by cultural and religious influences. They are also formed by your own experiences. For instance, a traumatic experience can shape a mental model that you will be hurt by people you love, making it hard to trust people and have good relationships. A child who never hears the word no learns that he is allowed anything he wants in life, and he becomes quite perturbed when people don't just give him what he wants in the adult world.

As you can see, many factors drive mental models, though they are not always helpful. Once a model has formed, it can be difficult to change, but it can be changed nevertheless. That is why educating yourself about mental models and learning to identify your own can help you figure out why you default to unhelpful behaviors, repeat the same mistakes over and over, or fail to make appropriate decisions and take calculated risks. Understanding your own mental models can provide the key to solving your life problems.

Unless you learn to identify and correct mental models, you will continue to use them for the rest of your life. This is not always a bad thing; for instance, continuing to stop at stop signs will prevent you from getting into accidents. But it can become a hurdle should you fail to rectify erroneous models or should you apply the wrong model to a situation that calls for a different one. Find the areas of life that you struggle with and then dig deeper to find the mental model that creates your struggles. These are the mental models you must change or override with logical thinking.

Perhaps you like to play it safe and never take a risk, but in order to get a job you love, you must risk everything. This mental model has protected you thus far, so you rely on it fully. But now, your mental model can keep you from making a change, which thus blocks you from advancing into your dream job. Employing System 2 decision-making and ignoring mental models can be quite helpful in certain situations.

For another example, consider a person who now believes that he is not good enough because his childhood created that mental model in his mind. He continually defaults to this belief and he keeps winding up with women who cheat on him and being passed over for a promotion at work. He does not understand why rejection keeps happening to him and he cannot see that his mental model is making him engage in behavior that triggers these unfortunate things to occur over and over again. By recognizing and changing his mental model that he is not good enough, he can grow his confidence and begin to go after better things in life. He can change his life around simply by addressing an underlying belief that he holds about himself.

Chapter 3: Mental Models In Problem-Solving

When you have a problem, you must decide on a solution. The more immediate the perceived danger of the problem is, the more automatic the problem-solving process will be using System 1. While this is perfect for life-threatening events, it can be problematic when it comes to less lethal life decisions.

A mental model is just a simplified way of looking at a complex problem. It allows you to understand and reach an accurate conclusion more easily, expending less metabolic energy. While you may not realize it, you use mental models all the time, every day. For instance, when you leave your house to go to work, you don't need a map because you know the way; your mind has a mental model of the way to work and it helps you make rapid-fire decisions about where to turn and which street to follow to get to your destination. It cuts down on the time you must spend consulting a map and making careful plans for how to reach your destination.

Throughout the day, you make a series of automated decisions that really help you. These mental models make life easier. They are quite useful in that regard.

Now, consider when they are not useful. Take a situation much more complex than finding your way to work, such as overhauling your finances because you just lost a job. You have a mental model of how you want to live your life and your finances have thus far supported that model. But now, you must cut a few expenses, and that will interfere with your lifestyle. You must restructure the mental model of your lifestyle to fit your new budget. That can be quite painful for most people.

Life never has a roadmap. When it comes to caring for aging parents, raising children, or any of the other millions of unique problems that people face every day, there is no guide because people and circumstances are all different. Your mental models don't have a clear guide for how to navigate new problems and no one can give you advice that perfectly matches your situation; you have not internalized any sort of map on how to respond.

But your brain is quite stubborn and it believes that it has the answers. Based on mental models that work for other situations, it tries to apply the same model to a new, unique situation. But that model may not work.

Ultimately, the brain is lazy because it is hardwired to avoid change and work. We don't solve the right problems; we tend to solve the easiest problems. In some circumstances, people get distressed over problems and neglect to solve them because they don't know how and they don't have a mental model in place to help them. Taking some time to employ System 2 thinking and finding a solution is better than simply ignoring a problem that you can't figure out.

Better Problem Solving

As you read on, this book will discuss developing a mental toolbox to help you work around or work with mental models to attain the best results in life. For better problem solving, there are a number of mental tools that can help you. Instead of relying on simplistic mental models for complex problems, it is better to whip out other means of arriving at solutions.

The most helpful way to solve problems is to think outside of the box. Rochard Feynman won the Nobel Prize in 1965 for physics. He didn't accomplish this by being smarter than the next guy; he accomplished it by using a different method for doing integrals that he had taught himself [10]. Feynman provides a wonderful example for how you can use a tool that no one else uses to get results.

It is best to develop multiple ways of looking at a problem and multiple skills to cover all of your bases. If you consider a problem from only one angle or apply the same skill to a new task, you may miss a lot of factors or details that are important. You essentially blind yourself to all of the different realities inherent to each situation in life. Having only one way of looking at the world causes you to try to stuff all of your situations into one framework, which certainly is not possible. Stepping outside of one perspective to view a problem creatively is a fantastic way to break free of the traps mental models can create.

For instance, let's say you are a software engineer. You know coding quite well and you are confident in your abilities to code. Yet one day you encounter a unique program that wants to accomplish something you have never written before. You don't know how to solve this because the code you know does not fit this new framework. So, instead of giving up, you begin to research new coding methods and experiment. You ultimately find what works.

Or consider a marriage. Your spouse is unhappy with the way you have been communicating. You want to change but you don't know how else to communicate; you have a solid mental model for communication. So, you read some books on communication and find a few new ways to say the same things. You try these new methods on your spouse and you find something that works.

To solve a problem, take a break. Try to look at it from someone else's perspective and get a sense of how it affects him or her. You can also consider how to overcome hurdles by thinking of ways other people might work around the hurdles instead of giving up.

You should also perform research. Read books that

you don't normally read and expose yourself to lifestyles or ideas you don't necessarily agree with. This can show you a new way to approach a life situation that you never thought of before. Educate yourself on new skills, as well, to learn a variety of methods to accomplish the same result. That way, you have a large array of tools available and you can pick one that works best for a given situation.

Chapter 4: Decision-Making **With** Mental Models

With the wide variety of situations that occur in life, it follows that one mental model cannot cover everything that may happen to you. To make sound decisions, you absolutely must broaden your mental models and develop more tools to help you make good decisions. Furthermore, you must refuse to let a mental model drive logic out of your mind.

Variety Matters

Your thinking improves with the more mental models you have that apply to real-life situations. The more models you possess, then the likelihood raises that you have the right models to see reality and make wise decisions. If you try to fit everything in life into the same problem-solving and decision-making model, then you fail to make useful decisions.

When it comes to improving your decision-making

abilities, variety is crucial. You must learn to adopt new ways of thinking and new tools in order to adapt to each situation as needed. Since every situation is different, having more mental models available to choose from makes you more successful and efficient at life.

Unfortunately, it is human nature to accept what comes easily and ignore what requires some mental work. We kid ourselves that we have thought hard about something when really we just took the path of least resistance and defaulted to an old mental model. Because of confirmation bias, we tend to only accept the thoughts that reinforce what we already believe. Thus, we tend to follow the same old paths of thinking without question. We find it hard to be flexible and try out different mental tools.

It is imperative to think outside the box and try different tools for each situation. Look at a situation without emotion and consider what model you have that is most akin to the situation at hand. Then use the model. If it does not work, think of a new model.

For instance, you may have a model in place for when you encounter an angry customer at work. If that model does not work in calming the customer, you must resort to a different method of conflict resolution. You must admit that your old ways are not working and you must accept the reality that you have to adjust your approach.

In another example, you may have a model of how to handle your relationship with your ex. But now that you are in a new relationship, you must create a new model to handle this new person. Get to know the person and experiment with what works and what doesn't work to find new methods. Be flexible enough to acknowledge that your old model no longer works and you must develop a new model to be happy with this new partner.

Minimize Black And White Thinking

Many people have an oversimplified model, a System 1 model that ignores the ambiguity that is inherent to life. They think that if they make a decision, everything thereafter will be wonderful. If they make the wrong decision, everything will be terrible. This oversimplified model neglects to take into account the reality that good and bad things happen in equal doses, no matter what you do.

A decision can be easier if you rid yourself of this harmful model, which is also known as a cognitive dissonance [11]. Stop thinking that one decision is the right one and one decision is the wrong one. Instead, think that both decisions hold their fair share of possible pros and cons. That form of thinking is far more realistic.

You can then break down the decisions you are weighing with a pros and cons list. Numerically rate the pros and cons to see which ones are more impactful. One is for least impactful, five is for most impactful.

For instance, moving to a new area may offer you many pros, but the single con that you can't afford it carries a lot of weight because being house poor can seriously lower your quality of life. Staying where you are has various cons, such as a bathroom you hate and annoying neighbors, but these cons are not as serious.

Finally, tally the numbers next to the pros and cons to get an overall score for each. Usually, the decision with the lowest score of cons and the highest score of pros is the decision you should go with. But say the pros for moving are so high that it doesn't make sense to not move. The single con is problematic, but now you can work on a solution for it. Finding a way to afford this new place can eliminate the con and make all of the pros worth it. So when you get your score, consider how you can minimize or eliminate cons to make the most positive decision possible.

Often, it is helpful to look for alternatives to two decisions, as opposed to seeking to find the correct decision [13]. For example, if you are torn between moving and staying put, why not consider how you can remodel your current home to make it nicer without having to move? Or can you move to a different home that is more affordable? If two decisions come loaded with problems, consider an alternative decision.

Logic Vs. Emotions

Humans make decisions based on emotion [12]. Often, this emotion is driven by a mental model. If you feel that your needs are being violated according to your mental model of how you should be treated, you become angry. If you see a person who reminds you of an abusive ex, you automatically fear or hate that person because you have a mental model that people who look like your ex are bad people. The emotions can cause you to make decisions that are not really based on reality and that are not ideal for a situation.

Removing the emotion from a situation can help you rely less on the mental model and more on logic. You can weigh the pros and cons and see which decision makes more sense. It can also help you see what must be done, no matter how you feel about it.

Most facts are pretty useless in and of themselves [13]. After all, knowing that a duck has a bill is not useful, but knowing how that duck uses its bill and what a clipped bill can do to a duck's overall health is useful to a vet or duck farmer. You must take basic facts and apply them to the overall situation to see how they play into reality [13].

Therefore, always collect all the facts. Then construct a sort of map in your mind that reduces the situation into a form that your mind can process [13]. Spell out how one action will affect the whole situation compared to another. You may look back at similar experiences in your past, but be sure to consider how this situation is a little or a lot different.

Always see where ego is creating a blind spot [13]. Maybe you don't want to fix your marriage by apologizing because that hurts your ego to admit you were wrong. Maybe you don't want to admit that you need help on a project at work, so you end up failing at the task. When ego rears its head and prevents you from doing what makes the most sense, consider that your ego is not keeping you fed and happy. Let it go and do what will yield the best outcome, regardless of how much it hurts your pride. Act on competence and skills, not ego.

You should also employ thought experiments. This is where you analyze your history, learn from your mistakes, and figure out how that can apply to your new situation [13]. Say you have had the same fight with your mom in the past and you still haven't resolved the issue, then you can safely employ a new method of conflict resolution, with possibly better results. If you always lose your temper and make emotional decisions when you fight with your mom which in turn make her angry, you can step back and reign in those emotions in to take a calmer approach.

You are experimenting, so you may not get the ideal results the first time around, but at least you are no longer employing the same method over and over for the same bad results. You are making progress toward a new mental model that may actually work. As you keep tweaking it, you develop the best mental model possible and you can keep using it for the same situation in the future.

When you are pondering a decision, think of the long-term consequences, not just the short-term. First-order thinking considers what solves immediate problems without regard for future problems [13]. This can cause you to make an even bigger mess of things. I remember running into a patch of money problems in college, so I took out a title loan on my car. Sure, the loan helped me through that rough time, but the exorbitant interest rate created far more money troubles down the road. Most regrets we have in life stem from using first-order thinking, not second-order, which considers the long-term effects of decisions [13].

Many people operate on assumptions that they believe wholeheartedly to be true. The age-old saying, "When you assume, you make an ass out of you and me" is always relevant. You must never base decisions on assumptions. You must collect all of the information. A common assumption is when you think you know what someone is thinking or feeling. You can't possibly know that, so find out what the person is really thinking or feeling before you put an assumption into place.

Finally, try weighing the likelihood of something you fear happening [13]. If you fear that you will lose everything by starting your own restaurant, look into the failure rates of restaurants. What you see may scare you, so then you can work on a solution, such as creating an emergency fund or a fallback option should your restaurant fail. Don't let the fear prevent you from going after your dream, since some restaurants do succeed.

Always use statistics and logical calculations to justify fear, rather than simply fearing a possibility and refusing to act on your desires as a result. Then use logic to find solutions to your worst-case scenarios should they actually happen. It is helpful to view potential problems and worst-case scenarios as hurdles to contend with, rather than blockages to your goals. A contingency plan is always wise; refusing to move forward on a goal because you fear the worst is foolish.

Chapter 5: Factors That Define The Quality Of The Mental Model

A mental model is of high quality if it sufficiently addresses a problem and causes you to create a good solution. You want your mental models to be of high quality. However, not every high-quality mental model will be so high quality in different situations. That is why you must use variety and have a large array of mental models to select from in your mental toolbox.

The more skills and frameworks you possess, the more likely you will select the most high-quality model for any given situation. Enriching your mind with mental models is key to living your best life and avoiding mental model traps.

Consider a team of ecological experts who are studying the ocean. The marine biologists know a lot about marine bacteria and animals. The geologist understands the land under the ocean, earthquakes, and other such geological features. The chemist understands the chemical makeup of the water. All of these scientists understand a small part of the ocean, but their knowledge limits them. They must collaborate to get a complete picture about how biology, chemistry, and geology affect the ocean, and thus Earth, as a whole. Only then can they create a useful solution for oceanic environmental problems.

The same goes for your life. You may have the skills to offer a great picture of one slice of life. But you don't have the complete picture and so you are operating on limited information. The only way to work around that limited (and limiting) view is to employ various disciplines to all areas of life, giving you a better idea of what your life is really like. You may not be able to do all of this on your own, so you must be open to collaborating with other people for ideas from outsider perspectives.

That is why you might be able to give your friends

great advice when it comes to dating or work. Yet you are lost when it comes to your own life. You have a better mental model for your friends because you can see things they can't; when it comes to your life, however, your view is narrow. You have created blind spots by looking at your life in one single way and blind spots can be deadly.

Thus, to improve the quality of your life, you must improve the quality of your mental models. You must broaden your horizons, be flexible to change, develop new skills or knowledge, and invite collaboration with others. All of this requires letting go of some of your age-old beliefs and your ego. The process is much harder than it sounds, but it is worth every bit of effort.

Flexibility

To make a mental model high quality, you absolutely must be flexible. This is because life is fluid and nothing remains static forever. Being willing to tweak your mental models or adopt new ones helps you keep up with the turbulence that is inherent to life. That makes you an incredibly valuable family member, worker, and anything else you may be.

For instance, for a simple mental model like getting to work, your model may become challenged the day you encounter construction on your route and must take a different way. Rigid people will get stressed and even irrationally angry over such a small issue. Flexible people will rapidly think of a new route or whip out GPS to make it to work on time, with little stress.

Now take a much more complex problem. Usually, you find that a certain method works great at work. The day it does not, you can give up in frustration or you can simply swap out your mental model to tackle the problem from a new angle.

Being flexible spares you a lot of stress. It also makes you calm and competent in times of change. Because you are willing to try things differently as needed, you find yourself able to handle more problems from a more effective angle.

Competence

The circle of competence that you learned about before definitely applies to any and all mental models you may use. Operating from ego leaves you with lots of blind spots that can literally or metaphorically kill you. A high-quality mental model enhances your competence and allows you to use your wide range of skills, regardless of your ego.

Don't ever think, "I must do this because it's how I always do this." Also don't think, "I have to do this to save face." Instead, find the best solution or decision and do it, without thinking of how you look to other people.

Multidisciplinary Approach

Back to our example of several scientists looking at a small slice of the ocean's complex makeup, you can see that multiple disciplines are the most effective. But if you're not an ocean scientist, you may wonder how this could apply to you.

Take parenting. A mixture of experimentation, communication science, and child psychology can help you become a better parent. You must also learn to handle your own faults as a parent to avoid transferring them to your child, so the discipline of introspection and self-help applies.

Or take a romantic relationship. There is more to it than cheesy dates and sex. You must learn to understand the gender you are dating as well as the person's individual psychology. You must learn good communication skills and leadership strategies and conflict resolution.

Finally, take your job. You may have a specific skill set that applies to your job. But being able to whip out a new skill set, like Feynman, makes you more valuable. As a customer service specialist or salesman, you must learn techniques for interacting with the public and individuals. You must learn communication, conflict resolution, and teamwork skills. But you must also learn everything you can learn about the work itself and the skills that go into it. If you are a computer programmer, knowing a wide variety of codes and staying on top of new programming languages is imperative to staying relevant in your rapidly evolving field. If you are an architect, you must learn new architectural trends and principles. If you are a doctor, you should focus on learning new research and keeping on top of studies, since the medical world is constantly changing and updating.

Whatever your trade is, learn all you can about it and bring new skills to the table. And, of course, work on your soft skills for dealing with your co-workers, clients, and the like.

Inversion

Inversion is where you tackle problems from the opposite direction you normally would. This allows you a creative way to change your mental model and find a solution. It lets you step outside of your own perspective for a while to see things you may have missed.

A good example of inversion is when you are about to enter a job interview. You probably focus on the three things that will get you the job. But you can invert this and think, "What three things will definitely cost me the job?" Focusing on how to avoid looking like an idiot can help you tailor your behavior effectively to get the desired result – an offer of employment.

Another example is how you might fear opening your own business because you ask yourself, "What will happen to me if I fail?" This strikes you with fear and keeps you from making your dream come true. Now you can invert that thinking and ask, "What will happen if I succeed?" Think about what you do want, not what you don't want.

First Principles

We as humans tend to make things far too complicated. Then we get overwhelmed and don't have a mental model that can help us find a solution to any complex problem. Stripping away the extra complications is called first principles thinking. You boil a problem down to its few elemental truths and then work from there.

To make mental models high quality, you must simplify things. This is not good if you ignoring important parts of a problem. But it is very good when you are blinding yourself with tons of "What if" scenarios and needless complications.

Strip something down. For instance, if you want to leave a job, you may be engaging in a maelstrom of anxious thoughts about what may happen if you do and what if you can't find a job and on and on and on! On a piece of paper, write down the first simple fact: I want to leave my job. Then, underneath it, list your reasons why. Also, list other jobs you are qualified for and interested in. This helps you realize the truths that make leaving your job a good decision, or a bad decision.

The Pareto Principle

The Pareto Principle is a cool concept that recognizes how things in life are not evenly distributed [14]. For example, one percent of the world holds ninety percent of the wealth. Or eighty percent of Italy belongs to only twenty percent of the population [14].

Therefore, not all of your efforts will get all of the results and benefits you were hoping for. Some mental models you have only yield a small percentage of results, while others yield a lot of results. So, if you focus on using the ones that yield the best results, then you will get more mileage out of your efforts. You can stop wasting time on unhelpful mental models.

A very simplified example is how your route to work may be shorter, but it is actually more stressful and takes longer because of traffic. Ditch that mental model for a new mental model of a route that will get you to work with less traffic.

A more complex one might be anxiety. You tend to spiral in anxiety and make some screwball decisions. When you take a deep breath and calm down, you make better decisions. Therefore, it is wise to ditch the mental model that calls for an anxiety meltdown and always use the one that calls for you to calm yourself down. I had to apply this one to myself and I noticed that my quality of life drastically improved when I employed a mental model of calm and serenity in the face of grave decisions.

Chapter 6: Biases And Heuristics

Biases and heuristics are decision-making tools that simplify complex problems. People assume certain things are true, and then they base decisions on those assumed truths. Biases and heuristics are efficient in that they save time, but they lead to lots of errors and problems [15]. Abandoning them is ideal.

The human mind is not so great at understanding probability, statistics, or availability. When you read a technical paper full of statistics, the numbers are probably fairly meaningless to you. It can be very hard for the human mind to grasp the exact quantity of "thirty percent of the sample size," and it can be even harder for it to apply that quantity to a meaningful understanding of the implications.

Thus, the human mind tends to rely on small numbers. Maybe something worked for you three times, so you assume it is a great way to do things, even though there is no statistical evidence that your method is successful even fifty percent of the time [15].

Why would we use heuristics? The main reason is effort reduction. If you use less effort to arrive at decisions, then you have more energy for other things.

Also, sometimes heuristics are pretty accurate. Based on patterns you have learned over time, they can draw from a wide range of experiences and knowledge at lightning speed. In some cases, they are quite helpful.

Furthermore, many people use attribute substitution. This is where they employ a simpler question in place of a more complex one. The result is that they choose the wrong heuristics to make decisions because their brains assume the decisions are actually much simpler than they really are. This has been shown to be helpful – making something simpler and acting on limited information can sometimes generate better decisions. Why this is so is not entirely clear, but it probably has to do with the fact that the human brain can only withstand so much information overload before it shuts down. Heuristics prevent that from happening, as does attribute substitution.

Availability

When making a decision, you tend to rely on the first few things that pop into mind. This facts or data are readily available, requiring little mental energy expenditure. Thus, you love them and prefer them. Your base decisions on them, even though they only provide a tiny snapshot of the whole picture.

Furthermore, people tend to ignore the availability of other options [15]. Instead, they pick an option that pops into their minds first because it requires little metabolic energy to achieve. A bank robber may need cash so his mind jumps to the option of robbing a bank, rather than starting his own business or making money in some other way. But his decisions may just land him in prison for a long time.

To make a good decision, you must consider other options and other information that does not immediately come to mind. Some research and expert opinions can help. So can spending some time meditating on a decision to retrieve even more data from the depths of your mind in a quiet, concentrated atmosphere.

Regression To The Mean

People tend to engage in regression to the mean. For example, if you score well on a test, you may assume you will score well on others just because you do well on tests or you are smart. You think that one experience defines others. But in reality, the test may have been so easy for you because of a certain combination of factors, including what you ate for dinner the previous night, how much sleep you got, and so on. The next time you take the test, you are more likely to score more normally.

Never assume that one unusual score or result will dictate the likelihood of more such scores or results. Just because you do something really well does not mean you will every time. You are more than likely to resort back to the mean. Bank on the mean more than on good luck.

Affect Heuristic

The affect heuristic is where people make decisions based on a gut feeling [15]. They swear this gut feeling is true, when really they don't know the source of it. The gut feeling may stem from a bias that the person is not even aware of possessing.

For instance, if you hear about a cancer research team and your father died of cancer, you might become biased toward the team just because of the gut feeling of dread and grief you experienced upon hearing the word "cancer."

Heuristics and emotions drive biases. Hence, making a clear decision is hard when you are influenced by an affect that may not even relate to the actual object being considered. Your affect may be totally unique to you because of your background; an oncologist might get excited hearing the word "cancer research team" because his motive to effectively treat cancer is much different from your motive to avoid the pain it brings.

A gut feeling is not a reliable way to make decisions. You must ignore gut feelings and prefer more logical ones. Many people swear by gut feelings. For instance, the Internet abounds with stories of people who went out on dates with strangers or who were hiking alone at night and got terrible gut feelings of danger, only to learn later that the person they were on a date with was a serial killer or a mountain lion was on the hiking trail. The truth is that going on dates with strangers or hiking alone at night are both inherently dangerous activities and these people knew it. They may have also sensed danger due to signs, scents, and other stimuli they did not consciously recognize. Nevertheless, it was not their guts that saved them, but rather common sense.

Overestimation Of Randomness

People tend to misunderstand and overestimate randomness. Many people assume that life plays out randomly and they can't make predictions. However, everything in life is based on probability.

In a famous example, a roulette wheel in a 1913 French casino landed on black twenty-six times in a row. People assumed that it had to switch to red any time, so they lost millions of francs betting against black. Really, the probability stayed at fifty-fifty, as always.

More people than not believe that the sequence THTHTH when flipping a coin is more probable than TTTTTT or HHHHHH. But really, all three possibilities have equal probability.

Do not ever assume that things are random and do not try to create patterns that are not there. That is why people usually lose at bets. Understanding basic probability is a smarter way to determine the likelihood of events.

Representativeness

People tend to use representativeness [15]. This is where they sort people or situations into categories based on readily observable traits or facts. They don't bother to collect all of the facts and create new categories for ambiguous things because that takes too long. Thus, people can wrongly sort things into categories that don't actually make sense. This can lead them to treat people whom they judge as criminals poorly when in fact these people committed justifiable crimes, for instance. Or it can lead them to avoid great opportunities because of a bias their representativeness has created.

Consider when you rate people into two groups: Good and bad. You avoid perceived bad people at all costs, even when they try to do good. You become extremely disappointed and disillusioned when good people do bad things. You must stop sorting people into such black and white categories and accept that everyone has good and bad inside of them.

You should also consider more categories. In many cases, categories are helpful. But like Venn diagrams, most people fall in that gray area between. They cannot be sorted into one of two simple categories. So, create more categories. Then you have more realistic pictures of the people or things you are dealing with.

Anchoring And Adjustment

A lot of your decisions can be influenced by anchoring. When anchoring occurs, a simple number or fact stays in the forefront of your mind, and you adjust accordingly.

For example, when someone offers you an apple for five dollars, you might laugh and say you would not pay so much for an apple. The person then asks you to pick a price. You have five dollars set as an anchor in your mind, so you don't go too far from it in your adjustment.

Real estate agents will often show potential buyers the most overpriced house first so that others thereafter seem like good deals. Again, that first house's price creates an anchor in the buyers' minds.

It is far more reliable to find out something's true

worth in the current market before letting an anchor influence your offer. You want to make an offer based on value. That prevents you from overpaying for things or assuming that something has more value than it does.

A lot of people will think that the most expensive items are high quality or the priciest meals are the best. There is no probability supporting that this assumption is true. Therefore, don't make a decision on quality based on the price of something. Test out the quality or read reviews to find out for yourself. In fact, it is sound advice to always test out and find out things for yourself and never operate on impressions, suppositions, socially accepted truths, or other people's opinions.

Recognition Heuristic

When you recognize something or someone, you are more likely to trust it. Therefore, you can make some bad decisions based on false trust. ==You cannot assume that something or someone is good, just because you recognize them.==

A good example is when you are betting on horses. You are most likely to bet on the one you know. But it may not be the best horse.

Or consider when you are choosing a doctor. You see a few names of doctors you don't know and then one name you do know from church. You select that doctor, assuming he's the best since you know him. Yet maybe he has fifty malpractice suits against him and he's about to lose his license.

This is why people stick with brands or people they know, instead of exploring and reading reviews. They hate to make a change because the familiar is so much more comforting.

This heuristic is also why people rely on word of mouth or celebrity endorsements. When they see people they trust or at least thing they know recommending products, they feel more inclined to buy them. They may even forego research into the product.

Don't let this heuristic blind you. Do your research and look into things before you place your trust in them. Never assume that something or someone you recognize is the best.

There are many heuristics that influence judgment. But they have been found to be far less efficient at generating great decisions than rational choice theory, probability, or logic.

Rational Choice Theory

Rational choice theory employs exploring your options to find the one that best suits your personal interests. Using the data you have available, you can pinpoint the most logical and rational choice that will serve you. If you must choose between a car with great gas mileage and a car that will make you look cool while costing more in gas, you must weigh which car meets your goals. Do you place more significance on looking cool or saving money?

With some exceptions, rational choice theory can be quite helpful. It is limited in that you may not be considering all possible options or you may be overlooking a key detail in one of your options that makes it a clear good or bad choice. Thus, you must take care to employ creativity and inversion to explore all of your options. Do your research and have a firm understanding of your personal values.

Less-Is-More Effects

Believe it or not, even logic and rational choice theory are not always ideal because of the high amount of unknowns that can occur in life. For example, if you are planning a picnic, you may account for rain and ants, but not for a tornado or a killer bee swarm. Thus, making rational choices can fail in that you don't have all unknowns accounted for.

Heuristics are particularly helpful in cases of risk [16]. This is because you don't have time to gather all of the evidence to make a logical or rational choice. You must use a heuristic to drive a very rapid decision. When using heuristics, you tend to trade accuracy for less effort. This saves you time and energy and can be helpful in very uncertain situations where immediate action is required.

Less-is-more effect comes into play here. This is where people tend to make more accurate inferences and wiser decisions with less information to work with [16]. This interesting effect seems to work because people can become confused and overwhelmed by a high number of options and a high amount of information. If you are in an unknown situation, you may want to make a decision that seems logical from the little information you have. Computer simulations and various studies support the less-is-more effect [16].

Chapter 7: Most Used Mental Models

Your mind has a large series of mental models for different situations [17]. But it tends to resort to a certain one for each situation that it perceives as similar to one it has already encountered – even if the situation is actually entirely unprecedented. Cognitive biases explore some mental models that you default to in certain situations, which can pose challenges or lead to poor decisions.

I remember when I got my first post-grad job. Before I had only worked in fast food, so my mind assumed my new job would be similar. Of course, I knew I wouldn't be flipping burgers, but I assumed the hierarchy and policies and stress would be the same. I entered the job with the wrong attitude as a result, and I was in for a rude awakening about what corporate life is really like. After the adjustment period, I loved it, but I think it would have been a lot easier had I not entered the job with a fast food job mental model in my mind.

Here are some of the most common mental models that you use and how to recognize them. Most of these models are helpful in their own ways, though some can be restrictive. Learning to tell when you are using a model and how to adjust the model for maximum reward is crucial to a good life.

Confirmation Bias

Life is quite uncertain. Therefore, when you get an idea, you seek confirmation for it. Once even the smallest thing has confirmed it, you believe it wholeheartedly and reject all confirmation against it [17]. Furthermore, you tend to stretch or twist facts to confirm your idea. You don't bother to research or acknowledge conflicting or opposing views.

Consider the ongoing debate between climate change supporters and deniers. It is actually impossible to say who is right. Climate change believers use evidence of changing weather patterns to support their opinions, while deniers claim that these changes in climate are normal and part of the world's natural cycles. Both parties take scientific evidence and twist it to fit their agendas. Neither considers that the other party is right, or that both parties may be right to a degree, or even that both parties are wrong.

The problem here is obvious. If you twist facts to confirm a bias you have, you are blinding yourself to the truth. Furthermore, you are purposefully misusing facts and denying the real truth. You can make yourself look like a real idiot at best, and you can make a deadly decision that affects others at worst.

It is far better to calm your biases by being open-minded. Accept the ambiguity of life, where two people with opposing ideas can both be right or wrong at the same time. A wise man knows that he does not know the truth about anything; a fool thinks that he knows everything.

Before forming an opinion or perpetuating opinions that you were taught as a child, look at all the available facts and viewpoints. Find the one that makes the most sense to you, but also be willing to change if you are ever proved wrong. Don't argue yourself blue in the face to keep an idea alive that is clearly erroneous.

Disconfirmation Bias

Related to the confirmation bias, it hurts your mind to accept things against which you believe [17]. Thus, to keep your ideas intact from challenging evidence, you refuse to acknowledge things you don't believe.

Growing up, my mother believed that sunscreen causes skin cancer, and she never let me wear it. I entered the adult world with this idea and dismissed all studies proving that sunscreen is beneficial as "bad science, supported by money-hungry doctors." That's how determined I was to perpetuate a belief I had been taught, because that belief was comfortable. When a friend of mine developed skin cancer because he never wore sunscreen, I was forced to reevaluate my stance on the issue.

You can make some mistakes in life if you refuse to acknowledge things that challenge your beliefs. It is ideal to keep an open mind and at least entertain things you don't believe in. You may find the evidence convincing enough to make you let go of a belief.

Backfire Effect

Related strongly to confirmation bias, the backfire effect is where you cannot change anyone's minds because they are clinging to what they think to be true [17]. Even if you have overwhelming evidence to support your claims, others will refuse to acknowledge that evidence. They may even cling to their beliefs even more strongly now that their ideas are being challenged. It is a matter of safety and pride; people do not like being wrong.

This is why you cannot change someone's mind about a political or religious matter. You will find that convincing people is often futile. It is best to not try unless you must.

You must also recognize when you are doing this yourself. Be more open-minded and accept that you do not always know the truth. There is nothing wrong with being wrong.

Self-Serving Bias

When you do something well, you take all the credit for it, claiming that your skills and abilities got you success [17]. When you fail at something, you blame other people or circumstances [17]. We do this to avoid hurting our egos by taking responsibility for failures. Then we bolster ourselves by taking full credit for our successes.

An example is when you fail a test because your teacher is a jerk. Yet when you pass the test next week, you take all of the credit for studying hard. In truth, you failed the first test because you didn't study and the teacher is still the same, no matter what.

Assigning credit or blame falsely can lead to a lot of problems in life. It frankly blinds you to valuable learning experiences. If you fail at something, you can learn from your mistakes by seeing where you went wrong. If you did well at something, you should see what circumstances, people, and actions made the outcome favorable so that you can replicate those conditions and skills again.

The self-serving bias is not always inaccurate. Maybe you did miss that tennis score because of bad weather; maybe you did excel at a job interview because of the qualifications and skills you bring to the table. However, you should consider that both internal and external factors play a role in every failure and every success.

Fundamental Attribution Error

The fundamental attribution error entails an outward reflection of the self-serving bias [17]. When you screw up, you attribute it to some outside force beyond your control. When someone else screws up, you attribute it to an internal flaw.

For instance, if you are often late for work, you probably have a string of excuses. "Traffic was insane!" "My child is sick!" "I didn't set my alarm!" Yet if a co-worker is often late, you sneer and think, "That person has terrible time management skills."

You cannot possibly know what causes another person to fail. You may think you know, but you are not in that person's shoes so you really don't. It is a mistake to look so negatively upon others and think their mistakes are due to internal flaws. You must accept that a combination of external and internal factors can be attributed to everyone's failures.

Looking at life this way makes you a more compassionate and understanding leader, since you are able to accept and work with your subordinates' mistakes. It also makes you a better spouse and parent, because you are not so hard on and critical of your family. Finally, it makes you less cynical and more balanced in your outlook on life, which can make you happier.

Hindsight Bias

After a car accident or a mistake at work or a breakup, you beat yourself up. "I should have seen that coming!" Now that you possess the knowledge of what was to come, it seems obvious. You think that you should have known the outcome before, when you didn't have this information yet.

Hindsight is 20/20. But hindsight is pretty useless. You can learn from your mistakes, but you can't ever change the past. Remember that you didn't know then what you know now, so you couldn't possibly make the prediction of the outcome [17]. Don't blame yourself for not having all of the information necessary for an accurate prediction of the future. No one knows the future.

Dunning-Kruger Effect

Have you ever met someone who knows everything about nothing? This person may not be a mechanic, but because he performed an oil change once, he fancies himself an expert on cars. Or he may not be a doctor, but because he Googles everything, he thinks he knows better than doctors.

This is the Dunning-Kruger Effect at play. It is a bias where you see things too simplistically when you lack information, so you think that you know everything about the subject. On the other hand, if you know a lot about something, you tend to have less confidence in your knowledge out of caution.

It is best to never assume that you are an expert at anything. No matter how advanced you are in a field or a line of work, there is always more to learn. You can avoid making mistakes and looking like a fool by not pretending to know things you don't.

Reciprocity Model

You know those salespeople at the mall kiosks, who give you free samples? As you try the sample, they smile at you and make you feel obligated to spend your money at their business. Or maybe you have a friend who does you favors and later says, "Well, since I did such and such for you, can you do such and such for me now?"

Reciprocity is a principle where people expect something in return for what they do [17]. If you perform a nice act, you expect to be rewarded or paid back. If you accept help from someone else, you are expected to return the favor.

Reciprocity is not always a bad thing. It is a great tactic for sales. But it can set you up for a lot of disappointment when you are not rewarded or paid back for something you did. Understand that you may not always reap rewards from the good deeds you do.

Optimism/Pessimism Bias

When you are shopping for a house in a good mood, you are more optimistic about what you can afford and how much you like a place. If you are in a bad mood later, you become more pessimistic about your situation. Mood influences your outlook and your subsequent decisions.

This is why removing emotion from the equation is always ideal, as is avoiding black and white thinking. If you fantasize about how everything will be perfect after you do something, recognize that you are using a poor mental model and adjust your thinking to be more realistic. If you see only gloom and despair, try to find a silver lining somewhere. Life is never all good or all bad; it is always somewhere on the spectrum between the two. Keeping this fact in mind at all times will lessen the ups and downs of your moods and open more opportunities.

Negativity Bias

The interesting thing about the negativity bias is that it is quite similar to pessimism. However, it is a little different. When you engage in this bias, you tend to think that the worst possible outcome is so much more important than the best possible outcome [17].

I keep returning to this example of opening your own restaurant for a reason: it reflects many problematic mental models in our minds. If you want to take the risk of starting a business, the worst possible outcome is going under in a short period of time and losing a ton of capital and still owing on any loans you may have received. But the best possible outcome is making a lot of money and doing something you love, while being featured on a Guy Fierri episode or the cover of a food critic magazine. The worst possible outcome may seem so bad that you focus on it more than the best one.

It is better to use probability. What is the chance of you failing and the chance of you succeeding? If you do fail, what contingency plan can you set up to cushion your fall? Think positively and you will open more doors in life without letting fear run the show.

Optimistic Probability Biases

The optimism probability bias is the deadly concept of "It can't happen to me" [17]. Teenagers may text and drive, thinking that horrible accidents happen to everyone but themselves. A drug addict may think that he doesn't have a problem and won't overdose because that only happens to others.

Being positive is a good thing. But being optimistic to the point of assuming bad things only happen to others is pure folly. Always consider your risk for bad things just as high as anyone else's.

Occam's Razor

In most cases, the simplest answer is the best one. But this is not one hundred percent true in all scenarios. Sometimes, you must analyze data a bit more or gather more facts to make a good decision. If you think something is obvious, take a second to test your assumption and make sure the obvious answer is really the right one [17].

Furthermore, the more assumptions you make, the less probable your answer is [17]. So if you make something overly complicated, it is probably not true. Minimizing complications is imperative to making a good decision. Calmly explore the facts and your options and go from there.

Hanlon's Razor

Your new crush sends you a brief text and you think he must not like you anymore, when really he is driving and too busy to text lengthily. Your co-worker screws up again and you think he did it deliberately to get you fired, when really he was just exhausted. This is Hanlon's Razor. You attribute malice when there is another explanation, often carelessness or busyness.

This comes back on the conventional wisdom: ==Do not assume.== Do not automatically assume a person's intentions without finding out what those intentions really are for sure. Always be certain before you draw a conclusion about someone's actions.

Forer Effect

As humans, we went everything to be neat and tidy, fitting a pattern we can understand. When you don't understand something completely, you try to fill those holes with ideas that make intuitive sense, regardless of whether or not you have any evidence to support the validity of those ideas [17].

When you read a book, you may not understand all of it. You hold onto what does make sense to you and discard the rest, thus getting only half of the message contained in the book. You miss out on a lot of critical details and don't actually understand the content at hand at all.

This principle can be observed in politics all of the

time, where the words of any politician are taken out of context and misconstrued. A Republican may believe that what his representative is proposing for healthcare is great because it appears to uphold his idea of how the country should be run, while a Democrat gets up in arms because he believes anything the Republican representative says does not fit into his ideas of how the world should work. More likely than not, neither person understands the full implication of what the representative is suggesting and thus they are missing the actual reality of a new law. They vote without proper comprehension of what is going to happen.

If you find yourself filling in gaps with a logical or intuitive rationalization, you should recognize that this mental model is in action. It is imperative to step back and test your "gap fillers" with facts to confirm that they are correct. Never accept something that appears obvious or logical as fact unless you can prove it.

Declinism

Declinism is that annoying tendency of older generations to shake their heads at younger generations and say, "Back in my day, we did [insert activity] and things were better. What is the world coming to?" At one time rock'n roll was feared to be the death of a generation; in the 1990s, hip-hop became feared in the same manner. Back in the time of Socrates, he lamented that the written word would be the downfall of humanity, and now people are saying the same thing about phones and computers. Yet we are still here, despite the enduring popularity both musical genres and the invention of the written word and the Internet.

Humans tend to fear and resent change, so when times change, people cling to the past because it is comfortable and lament the decline of humanity with social change [17]. But change is not always bad. Few societal changes have the ability to bring down humanity as a whole. As times change, so do people. The world and humans are both incredibly adaptable.

Another thing people tend to forget is that each generation has had problems with crime, teen pregnancy, drug abuse, etc. There has never been a perfect generation, not even in the "good old days." Each generation has its merits and demerits. Humanity will be just fine, no matter what changes.

It is best to stop blaming arbitrary things for the decline of humanity and instead recognize that change is normal and society has always had its problems, no matter what. The world is not in decline; in fact, it has stayed about the same with its levels of corruption and violence throughout history.

Nudging

Something small but impactful will "nudge" you to make a decision [18]. For instance, you see two perfectly good pieces of fruit at the supermarket but one has a blemish, so you are more likely to pick the one without a blemish. Perhaps you have a choice between two urinals and one has a fly in it, so you are more likely to use the other urinal. At a restaurant, a dish that is "special," such as the chef's special or a dish that makes the particular establishment famous, is the one you are more likely to order and even pay more money for.

Nudges are usually so small that you don't even notice them. They direct you to make a choice without really considering the full and broad aspects of the choice. For instance, there is nothing wrong with that blemished fruit or the urinal with a fly in it and maybe you would like some other dish at the restaurant with a lower price tag even better. Think long and hard before letting a small nudge influence you. Does a small factor even matter in your decision-making?

Anchoring

An anchor is an arbitrary number that is set before negotiations [17]. For instance, a used car priced at $13,000 sets an anchor at $13,000. As you bargain, you tend to avoid varying too far from the anchor.

In a study, people were asked if more or fewer than sixty-five percent of African countries belong to the United Nations [15]. Most participants guessed percentages close to sixty-five percent when the real answer is one hundred percent. Throwing out this arbitrary percentage gave people an anchor that they were too afraid to stray from.

When you feel limited by an anchor, consider being bold and creative. You may not get the used car salesman to go much under thirteen thousand, but you can at least try. By deviating from the anchor, you might get the best deal possible.

End anchoring is a bit different. It involves seeing data on the highest and lowest ends of the spectrum, so you tend to try to settle in the middle. Consider when you are comparing plans for a membership. The cheapest plan seems too basic and the most expensive plan sounds like too much. People routinely settle for the middle plan to avoid the two extremes.

Forcing Functions

Forcing functions are often stressful events that force you to take action [17]. A forcing function may be a tight deadline, forcing you to work more expediently. Or it may be the threat of being fired if you don't take on a task. It may even be finishing an article on your laptop because you forget your computer power cable.

Forcing functions are efficient, but stressful. We all know how bad stress is for health. So, minimize stress and simply hold yourself accountable for your time.

Consider how you will suffer or lose out if you don't do something in time. The result is motivation to minimize procrastination and distractions.

Theory Of Constraints

This mental model is the one great leaders and entrepreneurs use to launch themselves into success. In this mental model, you identify the one thing that is constraining you the most, the one thing preventing your success at a goal [17]. Then you figure out how to minimize that constraint to get what you want.

Take the problem of launching your own company. The single biggest constraint entails finding funding for start-up costs. That can be a big one, but it is solvable. By exploring options, you can find a loan with a good interest rate or a family member willing to invest in your company.

Every goal has its hurdles. The key is thinking creatively about how to overcome each hurdle as it arises. It can be hard, but almost anything is possible with some dedication and effort.

The Tragedy Of The Commons

Consider a traffic jam. Because one man decided to text instead of paying attention to the light, he held up traffic for another light cycle. He served his own self-interests and thus let down everybody else, creating a group problem that ends up hurting him in the long run as well.

When people are working with limited resources, it only takes one person's selfish actions to betray the group as a whole. Making short-term decisions for yourself without considering the good of others will lead to problems [17]. Problems within the group will always create long-term problems for you that your short-term action cannot solve.

Consider everyone involved before making a decision. Also, consider the far-reaching consequences of any decision. You are not the only person on this earth so you must not let down everyone else.

Certainty Effect

At an old job of mine, my boss decided to give me a raise. I expected an hourly one, but he decided to give me a check for several hundred dollars every few months. I was confused by this, as paying me an extra dollar per hour would have actually saved him more in the long run and benefited me more as well.

Another example is when you are offered two discount plans at a coffee shop. You may get a free coffee, or one hundred percent discount, every five cups you buy. Or you could get a thirty percent discount on each cup every day. The latter discount actually saves you more money in the long run, yet you prefer the one hundred percent discount because it seems bigger.

It is always wise to do the math and figure out if one hundred percent is really better than smaller percentages. Humans tend to think one hundred percent is ideal because it is bigger [17]. Yet smaller percentages can add up much more quickly and become greater in the end.

Framing

Framing will get you every time [17]. The way terms are phrased can blind you, making you think that something is a good deal when it really isn't or something is a bad idea when it is actually a good one [17]. When the same thing is rephrased differently, you change your mind, despite the fact both phrases refer to the same thing.

A great example is when a doctor tells you to lose

weight. Multiple studies have shown that this is not an effective statement; in fact, it tends to make patients gain *more* weight. This is because "lose weight" is phrased as a loss and most people are averted to losses. When a doctor phrases this same thing as a gain – "You need to gain more muscle mass" or "You should become healthier" – patients are more likely to comply and actually shed pounds. Basically, both phrases are the same, but one focuses on loss and the other focuses on gain.

Another example is a study where people were given two totally conflicting political statements and asked to agree or disagree. "People should be allowed to speak out publicly against democracy" and the second was "The law should forbid people to speak out publicly against democracy." Interestingly, sixty percent of people agreed with the first and forty-six percent agreed with the second, meaning many people agreed with both [19]. How can you agree with two opposite statements? Because of framing!

To break this cognitive bias, you should mentally rephrase things spoken in terms of loss into terms of gain. Maybe you will lose weight by exercising but you will also gain health and muscle mass. When speaking to clients, family members, or patients, always phrase what you want in terms of gain to get results. Avoid phrases that suggest a loss in any way.

Time Discounting

In this bias, you might be offered a hundred dollars today or a hundred dollars in a month. Of course you opt for the hundred today. Yet if you were offered one hundred dollars a day and two hundred in a month, you will take the two hundred in a month.

Time discounting is where you neglect to think of the future in favor of an immediate reward now [17]. The only way you will postpone the instant gratification is if the future reward is obviously greater. Humans prefer instant gratification; it is human nature. This is why people love using drugs to relieve symptoms of mental or physical illness as opposed to doing work to heal themselves from inside out, and this is why starvation diets that promise rapid weight loss are more popular than ones that actually help you get healthy and keep the weight off for good.

Instant gratification may feel good in the moment, but it seldom pays off in the future. You must think long-term. Will today's pleasure lead to harmful future consequences? Will that one hundred dollars be more helpful in the future when you have a big bill due? If you can, be sure to select the option that brings the most future benefits and delay gratification. It is painful because it goes against human nature, but the most successful people in the world are good at delaying gratification for a higher future reward.

Decoy Effect

In a study, subjects at a movie theater were able to get a small bucket of popcorn for three bucks or a large one for seven. Most people choose the cheaper one because they don't need that much popcorn. However, when a decoy option for a medium bucket for six dollars was added to the menu, people tended to choose the larger and more expensive bucket.

Why is this? A decoy is an asymmetrical third alternative that is closer in price to the more expensive option [17]. Thus, people find the more expensive option more tantalizing and even reachable.

When faced with three or more options, depend more on what you need than what "looks good." If you don't want a large bucket of popcorn, don't buy one. It may be hard to recognize when a decoy is influencing your decision, but doing the math and considering what you really need helps.

Deterring Of Small Decisions

Sometimes, a simple fact makes you lose sight of reality [17]. For example, when you hit the store with a credit card, you are likely to spend more because the money is not directly visible to you. Meanwhile, when you go with cash in hand, it is physically painful to spend money you already have, so you spend less. Another example is when you go out to eat with friends. When you dine alone, you order cheaper food, but when you're splitting the check, you somehow perceive that you are spending less so you end up spending more on a fancier meal.

The best way around this fallacy is to carry cash. If you can't, at least physically write down your electronic account balance. That makes the money you have more physical, so you avoid spending it as freely.

Sunk-Cost Fallacy

In this fallacy of thinking, you tend to think that you don't want to waste money or effort by ditching something, even though it is no longer serving you [17]. For instance, you might have a gym membership that you never use, but you refuse to cancel it because you have already spent so much money on it. Or you might have a poor investment but since you have already spent a lot of money on it, you don't want to ditch it.

When something no longer serves you, it is weighing you down in life. It is continuing to suck your resources and energy will giving zero in return. It is important to take the emotion out of the equation and say, "Is this really serving me anymore?" If the answer is a clear no, don't worry about the effort and money wasted. By ditching the thing that no longer serves you, you save more money and effort in the future. Stop holding onto things that no longer add any benefit or gain to your life. This applies to expenses, businesses, jobs, relationships, and habits.

Survivorship Bias

When planning your new business, you only look at other businesses with the same model that survived and you completely overlook the ones that failed. When gearing up for a dangerous hike, you concentrate on the number of people who made it to the top and down again alive and ignore the statistics of people who have died or gotten injured. Basically, you conclude that something is safe or wise because of a handful of successful people [17].

However, this blinds you to the inherent risks and dangers of any decision. You should never let fear stop you, but you should be realistic about your chances of failure or danger. That way, you can make a plan to avoid ruin.

Ostrich Effect

Like ostriches who bury their heads in the sand, people tend to avoid seeing what scares them. An unfortunate reality may be easier to just ignore. Problems may be best left alone.

While your problems may scare or overwhelm you, they will seldom go away on their own. It is best to face problems head-on and solve them. Letting them fester on their own will often make them worse. So if you feel sick, go to the doctor. If your marriage is failing, go to couples counseling. If you need help on a work project, ask for it now rather than later. Taking proactive steps in life can help you mitigate or even solve problems before they become too big to handle.

Salience

This is where you focus on a more dramatic or obvious idea than a statistical likelihood. For example, you may fear flying because you are terrified of crashing, yet you don't mind driving. Yet you are statistically far more likely to die in a car accident. Driving more safely and owning a car with better safety ratings would be a logical choice, but instead you focus on avoiding planes.

This is also a large reason why people may go for the partner who is the most attractive. They don't look for more enduring traits, such as loyalty and reliability and honesty. They see one glaring trait in a person and make judgments based on that.

Instead of looking at the most obvious or dramatic fact, look at what really matters. What fits into your values? What has a higher probability of happening? Use this to make informed choices and conquer fears.

Placebo Effect

You probably already know this from medicine. You

give someone a sugar pill and say it will make him sleepy. Ten minutes later, he is sound asleep. The human mind has the remarkable ability to make what it believes to be true.

The placebo effect goes on to cover other areas of life, however. If you think something will happen, you engage in small subconscious actions that make it happen. However, if you eradicate harmful suppositions about the future, you may be able to mitigate this effect.

Recency

What is going on now tends to override the probability of change. You value newer information over old information. For example, you may assume the stock market will always be this way so you make short-term decisions that don't endure with the market's inevitable changes.

Don't rely too much on newer information. Consider the past and predictions for the future to make a more informed, wholesome choice.

Pro-Innovation Bias

Has your boss ever become a little too excited about some new innovation and pushed it on everyone, even though it was problematic? In pro-innovation bias, you tend to overvalue something's usefulness to ignore its limitations. This is why companies excitedly roll out new features and push how great they are, while downplaying their limitations and problems.

People tend to do this in all areas of life. If you are moving, you play it up and claim that it will solve all of your life problems. You fail to see the reality that moving will come with its own problems. Moving may still be the best choice, but it won't fix your entire life for you.

You must not let something's usefulness or novelty cloud your judgment. Be realistic about its limitations. Look at the big picture. Then you can tell if something is really useful or actually useless.

Clustering Illusion

Many people see faces in wall stucco or notice patterns in crowds that aren't really there. The tendency to see patterns that do not exist fool us into thinking that we can make a decision based on a pattern. But if this pattern is false, then we can make the wrong decision.

Consider when you have encountered a pattern where you become successful at work during summer, and then your productivity declines during winter. This has happened two years in a row. From that small sample size, you believe that you will have the same experience again so you reschedule all big projects for summer and take it easy all winter. Except the pattern does not continue; you are distracted and busy all summer and thus your productivity declines.

It is best to not rely too much on your perceived patterns. The odds of them being false are quite high. Do not assume that a pattern will sustain, either.

Chapter 8: Cognitive Dissonance

It is difficult to honor two opposing ideas in your brain at the same time. In fact, it is almost painful for the brain. A cognitive dissonance is the clash you feel when you see two opposite ideas and you must decide for yourself which one to follow or you must modify your behavior to return to a state of comfort [20]. You may know one thing, but you act differently, and this can be distressing.

Take smokers. While smokers know that their behavior is quite bad for their health, they do it anyway. They often feel guilty about smoking, or they find ways to justify it like "I am just so stressed right now." The problem here is that smokers are experiencing a cognitive dissonance between knowledge and behavior.

Another example is when a person claims that he doesn't believe in infidelity, yet he cheats all of the time. He is probably genuinely against infidelity but his behavior makes him appear like a hypocrite. He probably experiences pain due to this cognitive dissonance and he finds many excuses to justify his poor behavior and thus minimize the painful guilt in his mind.

When you encounter cognitive dissonance, you feel extremely unsettled [20]. You must change something to reach a state of comfort again. You might do this by modifying your behavior and beliefs, but since people like to cling to their behavior and beliefs due to confirmation bias, it is far more likely that you will twist facts or find some excuse to justify the cognitive dissonance.

Back to the example on smokers. Since they don't enjoy the cognitive dissonance, they may quit smoking. More likely, however, they will use disconfirmation bias to claim that science is overexaggerating, or they will use optimistic probability bias to convince themselves that they will not get lung cancer.

Change of any kind is hard. That is why people have the amazing ability to ignore facts, make excuses, and even use the ostrich effect in order to ignore the truths that cause their cognitive dissonances. They can keep the same behavior and avoid change, without allowing the discomfort of challenging beliefs.

Cognitive dissonance is a powerful motivator [20]. Some people barely feel it because the cognitive dissonance challenges a belief or behavior they are not too attached to, or it does not challenge a belief or behavior terribly much. Other people find cognitive dissonance intensely unpleasant because they cherish a certain belief or behavior. People will react accordingly to their states of dissonance to reach a state of internal balance that appeases the cognitive dissonance [20].

Beliefs about the self are the most powerful sources of cognitive dissonance [20]. Imagine the pain you feel when you think you are a good person and someone calls you a bad person and has evidence to support their statement. You find your self-esteem wounded and you struggle to make peace with yourself again. It can take a while to heal from such a blow.

You may also get irrationally angry when someone challenges the beliefs that shape your existence [20]. If you were raised Christian and you follow the faith, you will not take kindly to evidence that challenges the validity of your religious texts or the existence of Christ. You will do anything to somehow dismiss this evidence to maintain your faith. This is when you see people claim that dinosaur fossils are fake because evolution challenges their theories of Christian creationism.

Finally, the ration between clashing thoughts and consonant thoughts set your discomfort level [20]. If you try to be one person but you constantly think, "This is not me. I need to change," then you are experiencing a high level of uncomfortable cognitive dissonance. You are feeling it so much that you probably attempt to either change yourself or you engage in distracting behaviors. On the other hand, if you occasionally think that maybe your job isn't for you but then you experience other thoughts about how much you love your job, your rate of cognitive dissonance is much lower. You are able to stay at your current job and handle the unpleasant aspects of it.

What To Do

When you experience cognitive dissonance, you can become incredibly confused. Your mental models are being challenged and thus your idea of how to live life is shaken. That can be disconcerting even to the strongest, most mentally fortified person. It is imperative to restore balance by addressing the dissonance head on, rather than burying your head in the sand or making up flimsy justifications.

The best thing to do is to compare the weight of the rewards between modifying your behavior and staying exactly the way you are. For example, if you are eco-conscious but you drive a gas hog, you can either get an eco-friendly car or you can minimize your emphasis on the environment. Which behavior means more to you and offers you a greater reward? To a person who loves his car or can't afford another one, the latter option would offer a greater reward. To someone who truly does value the environment, the former option is obvious.

The second thing to do is to consider that you are not looking at the only two truths. Is it possible that evolution and creation both occurred? Is it possible to find new stress relief and quit smoking, or somehow minimize the bad effects of smoking or cut down on how much you smoke every day? No one has the answers to everything, but you can probably find one that works for you. Compromising two conflicting beliefs can help you find a happy medium where you can achieve consonance, or peace.

Always do your research to uncover new options or effectively discount one of the beliefs that triggers the dissonance. Thousands of studies say that smoking is bad, but several say that nicotine is good and only the other ingredients in cigarettes lead to cancer. Thus, with that information, you can find a way to ingest nicotine without smoking.

You can work on reducing the importance of one of the conflicting beliefs. Find which one matters to you the most. Consider if you are placing importance on something for frivolous reasons. If you are holding onto a belief or attitude to impress or please other people, for example, then you can safely minimize the importance you place on that belief.

Forced Compliance

You are forced to do something publicly that you really don't want to do privately. This creates a huge dissonance that can be quite jarring. If you are forced to apologize for something you are not sorry for, you feel a dissonance.

After an incidence of forced compliance, you must make peace with the past to get any consonance. Thus, you must either justify what you did or reduce the importance of your private values. Which option is better for you personally?

Decision-Making

Another huge source of cognitive dissonance involves making a decision [20]. If you must choose between two evils, you find that both decisions go against your idea of how things should be. How do you make the best decision?

Usually, it is best to weight all aspects of both decisions and then decide which one will cause you the least harm. You should also consider how harmful a perceived harm is. For example, if you must choose between a house with a tiny kitchen and a house with a tiny bathroom, neither is particularly life-threatening. So you must make the decision based on whether or not you cook or need lots of room for a makeup arsenal.

On the other hand, if you must choose whether or not to pull the plug on a loved one on life support, both decisions carry significant heartbreak and harm. You know that you will grieve terribly if you let your loved one die, but you also know that he will never have quality of life again and the financial burden of keeping him on life support is much more harmful in the long run than experiencing grief.

To avoid tragedy of the commons, you should take others into consideration. What do other people feel about this decision? Will they be affected? If they will be affected, then their input matters. If they won't, then you need to make this decision independent of what they think.

Effort

If you spend eight years creating a masterpiece and it doesn't turn out to your satisfaction, you feel incredible cognitive dissonance. If you spend lots of money, you want to be sure that you will like the product or else you will feel intense pain and loss. Thus, you want to put lots of effort or resources into something that you consider worthwhile and you want to avoid regrettable decisions or wastes.

The best thing to do is to consider perceived wastes as beneficial somehow. Maybe you "wasted" ten years with a person and now you have broken up. It is helpful to minimize cognitive dissonance about how much time you squandered by considering how the relationship helped you grow as a person and how you were content for some of that time. Or if you spent lots of money on something, you can consider how you can sell it and make at least some money back.

Try to minimize the perception of wastes. You did something at one time for a reason. If it didn't turn out as desired, that is OK. You gained something out of it. Be sure to cut out things in your life that no longer serve you instead of clinging to them out of sunk cost fallacy. That fallacy only increases the level of cognitive dissonance over time.

Chapter 9: Reversible Vs. Irreversible Decisions

Some decisions have little weight on life and can be changed, or reversed, easily. For instance, ordering the wrong thing for lunch is an easily reversible decision because you have many choices that can be changed. But some decisions are weightier and more complex. They impact your life and once you make them, you cannot go back. Selling your home and moving across the country is an irreversible decision; quitting your job is another type of irreversible decision.

A reversible decision is easy to make because you can always back out later on if you make the wrong choice. But a lot of decisions in life are not so simple. Once you make it, you are committed to the consequences. Being prepared for consequences of every decision you make helps you avoid being blindsided and making the wrong choice. You should never make any decision lightly, even if it is reversible.

When it comes to making irreversible decisions, you had better be sure! That fact can be quite scary, as you fear you will make the wrong decision. You can become frozen in a sort of decision-making limbo, terrified of the possible negative consequences of either decision. This can prevent you from seeing what you must do clearly.

It so follows that humans are biased to make irreversible decisions using consonant information [21]. In other words, you make the decision that aligns most closely with your personal values and things you think to be true. Dissonant, or challenging, information is scary and thus you avoid it when making irreversible decisions. This is not always so in the case of reversible decisions.

When faced with an irreversible decision, you must slow down. This is what Jeff Bezos always does and you can see where he is today. Slowing down lets you weigh all options and find the most consonant ones. Then you can make a decision that fits into your mental models and meets your individual needs.

Before you even make a decision, ask, "Is this reversible or irreversible?" It is definitely acceptable to adopt different decision-making techniques for either one.

For reversible decisions, you can rely on basic mental models and take some risks. This does not mean that you should be foolhardy and do reckless things. It means that you can try out a new restaurant despite your lack of experience with it because it doesn't matter if you hate the restaurant or not. It means that you can experiment with a new hair color because you can change it if you don't like it.

For more uncertain and irreversible decisions, it is important to get a good sense of your own values. Only then can you tell what matters enough to you to take a risk. If you want to work in a certain field but you're not sure if you will like it, you can weigh the importance of the work versus how much you enjoy your current career. Will staying in your current career fulfill you? Or is it worth the risk of not liking a new career to change?

Becoming frozen in a web of doubt and confusion is hardly conducive to anything. When you become paralyzed by choices and doubt, you can't see clearly. Make things as simple as possible and remove all "What if?" scenarios in your mind. Then research your options. The best decision will become clear to you then.

Think Outside The Box

Your mind is far more than just your brain and its tissues. It is a collection of inherited traits, environmental boundaries, learned behaviors, conditioned responses, and biases. It is shaped by the things we have found out for ourselves and the things we have learned in school.

Inside our own minds, we feel safe. This is why we cling to the ideas we hold because we know them. New ideas and the outside and the unknown are all quite scary. These things carry a lot of inherent risk.

Thinking outside of the box is a combination of all these things that scare us.

How do we go out of the box? We need to add divergent information that challenges what we assume to be true. We must be willing to break down boundaries that we have learned and asked questions we have never asked. We must explore facts that we disagree with and listen to people with alternate perspectives to our own. We must apply principles we have learned to new areas of life and we must consider probability over our own emotions. At times, we must try things that we never have before, running a sort of life experiment. And we must be willing to try new things, meet new people, and push our limits.

Long-term thinking takes you far. When it comes to an irreversible decision, never just consider what may benefit you in the present moment. Think of how you will feel in the future and what future benefits you may reap. Investors do this. They spend some money now in order to see their wealth grow in the future. The initial investment may hurt because they don't just go buy a bunch of cool stuff with the money, but the long-term rewards are rich.

Therefore, try to think how this decision will impact you in a year, five years, ten years, and so on. For example, if you are switching careers, compare health benefits and retirement because those things matter in the end far more than feeling excited to get up and go to work in the morning. Most jobs are problematic and boring at some stage, so you can't expect to be happy every day of work. You can, however, be happy when you retire and don't have to work at Walmart part-time.

Look for alternatives and not just the correct answer. When you seek the correct answer, you often narrow yourself down to two options. But life has so many options that you could overlook the best one as you pressure yourself to find the correct one.

Mathematicians are notorious for this. Most people think that math is straightforward- there is only one right answer. But in more complex and theoretical mathematics, there may be several right answers, or the right answer is not known or testable. Thus, these guys will employ interesting new theories and solutions to reach answers that no one ever imagined before. They are willing to explore alternatives to existing theories and challenge answers that are accepted to be true.

Furthermore, look at the motives behind why you are leaning toward a certain decision, or what is making you feel confused. For example, maybe you were taught not to take risks as a child, so now the idea of quitting your job to open a business terrifies you and you hold yourself back. When you find the underlying building blocks of your mental models, you can see where irrelevant life experience is now influencing you. You can strip that experience away and focus on the bare facts and the present motivations you have.

Don't rely too much on the past. Yes, the past is a valuable source of lessons and information to protect us in the future. But in many cases, we only assume things will work out just as they did in the past. That makes us fearful and we create a self-fulfilling prophecy of sorts [21].

For example, when I first met my wife, I was terrified of meeting her parents because my last girlfriend's parents hated me for no apparent reason. I was extremely nervous and this made me act like a buffoon. My future in-laws did not like me as a result and I was convinced that there was something intrinsically wrong with me to make parents hate me. However, in time, I managed to prove myself to them and we have a good relationship now. I assumed the past would repeat so I created a self-fulfilling prophecy.

Never let the past butt into the present. If you made a mistake before, ponder what you did wrong and ensure that you don't do it again. That doesn't mean you should never try the same thing again. Maybe times will be different, especially now that you are armed with more information from past failures.

You can ask for more time if you need. Never be afraid to ask for more time. Sometimes, life moves more quickly than we can keep up and a new job offer or a house you want to make an offer on slip out from under you. In that case, you can tell yourself "It wasn't meant to be." Only when you feel confident in a choice should you make it.

A final great thing is that the less information you have, the better your plan can be [19]. The mind has an amazing ability to make safe decisions in the face of limited information. So, when you are weighing two options in an irreversible decision, go with the decision that seems most logical without overanalyzing it. While you should take your time to think over alternatives and research, you will ultimately have a preference. If this preference tests out and the decision seems sound, don't let doubt infiltrate your mind. Just pounce on the decision that you like best and make it.

Now as you can see, mental models are both helpful and harmful. Some need to be overcome. When you feel trapped by a mental model, you need to find ways around it to open up your life and make better choices. This topic will be covered extensively in the next book, *Mental Model Traps.*

Conclusion

Mental models are great ways to streamline decision-making and problem-solving, but they can be problematic. Relying on mental models too heavily is not ideal. Instead, you must use logic and create high-quality mental models to make life work for you.

Mental models are your mind's maps of the world. Some mental models are unique to the person; others are fairly universal cognitive biases and heuristics that influence most people when making decisions. Recognizing when you are using a mental model (in other words, all of the time) helps you tell if your thinking is rational or influenced by some driven track in your mind.

Mental models are created by so many different factors. Thus they are unique to each person, and impossible to fully understand in other people. You may not even understand your own. This is why you cannot trust your intuition. Rely on probability and logical facts more. Intuition is often a lie that your brain tells itself, based on mental models that lie beneath your consciousness.

It is more than possible to adjust mental models as needed. Perhaps you engage in an optimistic probability bias and you think your chances of survival are higher than the average person's when you take a risk. It may save your life to step back and realize that your chances of incurring harm or dying are just as high as everyone else's. Learn to employ the right mental model at the right time and your life will become both safer and more fulfilling.

Mental models are most important when you are solving problems or making decisions. Finding the most logical choice or solution is more foolproof than relying on "intuition." Intuition is often wrong, as it is driven by hidden mental models you are not even aware of. Logic and rational choice theory are far better ways of making decisions and solving problems in life.

As you begin to employ these new mental models to your life, you will notice everything improve. You are no longer trapped in the narrow scope of mental models that do not serve you in all situations. Instead, you are able to choose what is best at all times. This makes you excel in work, sports, school, and relationships. You will become a leader and inspire others to trust you.

Many factors go into creating more high-quality mental models that serve you better in all areas of life. Having flexibility is one key. Another key is to remove assumptions and emotions from your thinking, as both cloud your judgment and lead to poor or irrational decisions.

Now that you understand mental models and the common ones you use, you are prepared to restructure your thinking to be more beneficial. You have the tools to create excellent mental models and switch them out as required. It is up to you to employ these tools to drive the results you want from life. When you do, you will find yourself reaping the maximum benefit from all areas of life as you make excellent decisions and solve your most perplexing problems.

It is critical to start today. A high-quality mental model for every situation and a huge toolbox of mental models will get you farther than relying on the same few problematic or distorted ones. Don't wait any longer to start making great decisions.

Do you want to...

⇒ Stay up to date and hear first about new releases?

⇒ Get huge discounts and freebies?

⇒ Improve your thinking and have more success in life?

Sign up for our newsletter and get our thinking cheat sheet as a free bonus! Inside you'll find: 21 timeless thinking principles you need to know to upgrade your thinking and make smarter decisions (not knowing these may hinder you from having the success you'd like to have in life)

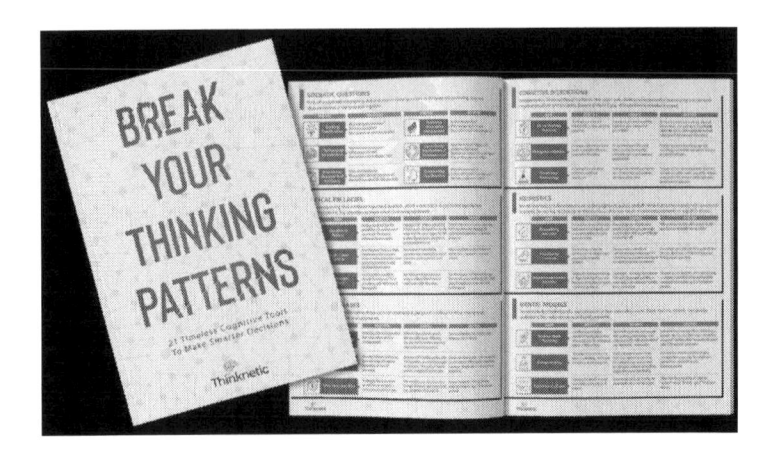

CLICK HERE TO DOWNLOAD FOR FREE!

Or go to www.thinknetic.net or simply scan the code with your camera

References

1. Forrester, Jay. Counterintuitive Behavior of Social Systems. 1971.

2. Craik, Kenneth. The Nature of Explanation. 1943.

3. World Bank. Thinking with Mental Models. http://pubdocs.worldbank.org/en/504271482349886430/Chapter-3.pdf.

4. Johnson-Laird, Philip & Byrne, Ruth. Mental Models or Formal Rules? Behavioral and Brain Sciences. Vl 16, No 2, pp. 368-380. 1993.

5. Krawyczyk, Michal. Unforced Errors: Tennis Serve Data Tells Us Little About Loss Aversion. Econ Journal Watch. Vol 16, No 1. March 2019.

6. Kahneman, Daniel. Thinking: Fast and Slow. Farrer, Strauss, and Giroux. 2011. ASIN: B00555X8OA.

7. Ranganathan, VK, et al. From Mental Power to Muscle Power: Gaining Strength by Using the Mind. Neuropsychologica. Vol 42, No 7, pp. 944-956. DOI: 10.1016/j.neuropsychologia.2003.11.018

8. Evans, Jeffrey & Meyer, David. Executive Control of Cognitive Processes in Task Switching. Journal of Experimental Psychology, Vol 27, No 4, pp. 763-797.

9. Watson, J. B., & Rayner, R. (1920). Conditioned emotional reactions. Journal OF EXPERIMENTAL PSYCHOLOGY, 3(1), pp. 1–14.

10. Feynman, Richard. Surely You're Joking, Mr. Feynman! 1997. W.W. Norton & Company. ISBN-13: 978-0393316049.

11. Huffman, AJ. Cognitive Distortion. 2011. CreateSpace Independent Publishing Platform. ISBN-13: 978-1466351363.

12. Lerner, Jennifer, et al. Emotion and Decision Making. Annual Review of Psychology. Vol 66, pp. 799-823.

13. Parrish, Shane. The Great Mental Models: General Thinking Concepts. ASIN: B07P79P8ST.

14. Pareto, Vilfredo. The Rise and Fall of the Elites. Bedminster Press. 1968. ISBN13: 9780405121104.

15. Tversky, Amos & Kahneman, Daniel. Judgment Under Certainty: Biases and Heuristics. Oregon Research Institute. 1973. Retrieved from: https://apps.dtic.mil/dtic/tr/fulltext/u2/767426.pdf.

16. Katsikopoulos, KV. The Less-Is-More Effect: Predictions and Tests. Judgment and Decision Making. Vol 5, No 4, pp. 244-257. 2010.

17. Nantchev, Adrian. 50 Cognitive Biases for an Unfair Advantage in Entrepreneurship. 2016. ASIN: B01M34BW42.

18. Thaler, Richard & Sunstein, Cass. Nudge: Improving Decisions about Health, Wealth, and Happiness. 2008.

19. Plous, Scott. The Psychology of Judgment and Decision Making. 1993. McGraw-Hill. ISBN: 978-0070504776.

20. Festinger, Leon. A Theory of Cognitive Dissonance. 1957. ISBN-13: 978-0804709118.

21. Frey, Dieter. Reversible and Irreversible Decisions: Preference for Consonant Information as a Function of Attractiveness of Decision Alternatives. Personality and Social Psychology Bulletin. Vol 7. Issue 4. 1981. https://doi.org/10.1177/014616728174018.

Disclaimer

The information contained in this book and its components, is meant to serve as a comprehensive collection of strategies that the author of this book has done research about. Summaries, strategies, tips and tricks are only recommendations by the author, and reading this book will not guarantee that one's results will exactly mirror the author's results.

The author of this book has made all reasonable efforts to provide current and accurate information for the readers of this book. The author and its associates will not be held liable for any unintentional errors or omissions that may be found.

The material in the book may include information by third parties. Third party materials comprise of opinions expressed by their owners. As such, the author of this book does not assume responsibility or liability for any third party material or opinions.

The publication of third party material does not constitute the author's guarantee of any information, products, services, or opinions contained within third party material. Use of third party material does not guarantee that your results will mirror our results. Publication of such third party material is simply a recommendation and expression of the author's own opinion of that material.

Whether because of the progression of the Internet, or the unforeseen changes in company policy and editorial submission guidelines, what is stated as fact at the time of this writing may become outdated or inapplicable later.

This book is copyright ©2019 by **Joseph Fowler** with all rights reserved. It is illegal to redistribute, copy, or create derivative works from this book whole or in parts. No parts of this report may be reproduced or retransmitted in any forms whatsoever without the written expressed and signed permission from the author.

Printed in Great Britain
by Amazon